THE 12 DISCIPLES OF JESUS

BOOK ONE

WRITTEN BY
TEMALESI W.M.K. SAVOU

ILLUSTRATED BY
BETHANY WHITWELL

Copyright © 2017 by Temalesi W.M.K. Savou. 764582

ISBN: Softcover   978-1-5434-0312-1
       Hardcover   978-1-7960-0999-6
       EBook   978-1-5434-0311-4

Print information available on the last page

Rev. date: 02/13/2020

To order additional copies of this book, contact:
Xlibris
1-800-455-039
www.xlibris.com.au
Orders@Xlibris.com.au

INTRODUCTION

When Jesus who is our Lord and Saviour was here on earth he chose twelve men to be his helper. Jesus called them 'DISCIPLES'.

PETER

This is Simon who is called Peter.

He is a Fisherman.

Peter has a fishing boat.

He loves to go fishing everyday in his fishing boat.

Peter would take his fishing rods and his fishing nets when he goes out fishing so that he could catch a lot of fishes.

Whenever Peter catches a lot of fishes
he would sell them at the market.

One day a man named Jesus was walking by the sea of Galilee.

He saw Peter throwing his big fishing nets into the water.

Jesus said to Peter, "Follow me, and I will make you fishers of men".

Peter immediately left his nets and his big boat and followed Jesus.

Peter became Jesus' first disciples.

ANDREW

This is Andrew.

Andrew is a very strong fisherman.
He loves to catch big fishes.

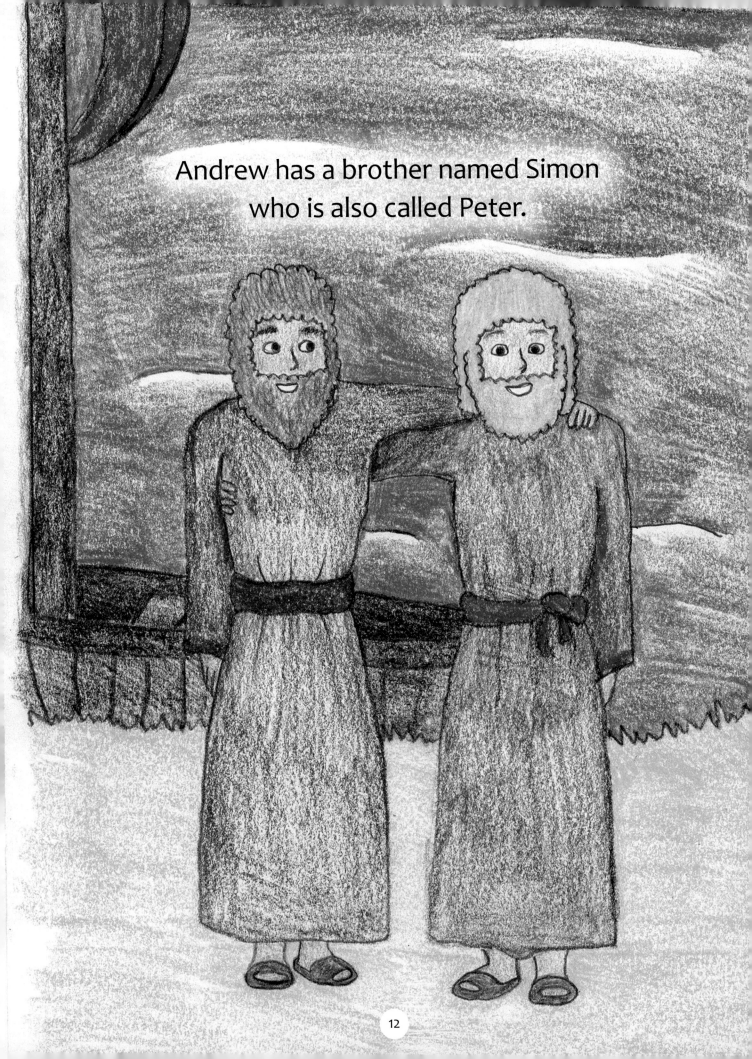

Andrew has a brother named Simon
who is also called Peter.

Andrew and Peter loves to go fishing together in their big boat.

Andrew and his brother Peter would
catch a lot of big fishes.

Andrew would sell the fishes he catches
from the sea of Galilee in the market.

Andrew has a best friend. His name is Jesus. He calls Jesus the "Messiah".

One day as Jesus was walking by the sea of Galilee, he saw Andrew and his brother Peter throwing their nets into the sea.

Jesus was happy to see them, and he called out to Andrew and Peter, "Follow me and I will make you Fishers of Men".

Andrew and his brother Peter immediately left their nets and followed Jesus.

Andrew was the second disciples of JESUS.

JAMES

James is a fisherman.

He lives with his parents and his younger brother.

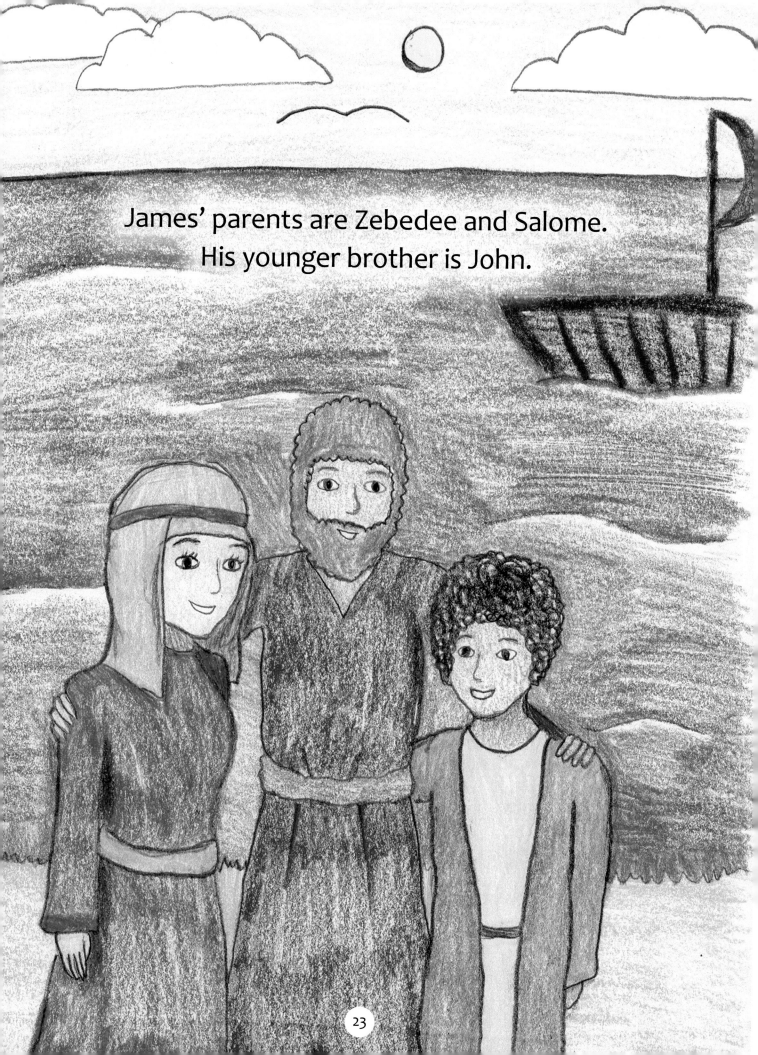

James' parents are Zebedee and Salome.
His younger brother is John.

Everyday James would go fishing with his father and his younger brother. They always enjoy going fishing together.

They would catch lots of different types
of fish with their fishing nets.

James would accompany his father and his younger brother to the market where they would sell the fish they catch.

James' mother Salome, would help them in the market too.

James has an aunty named Mary. Sometimes
James would share some fish to his aunty Mary.

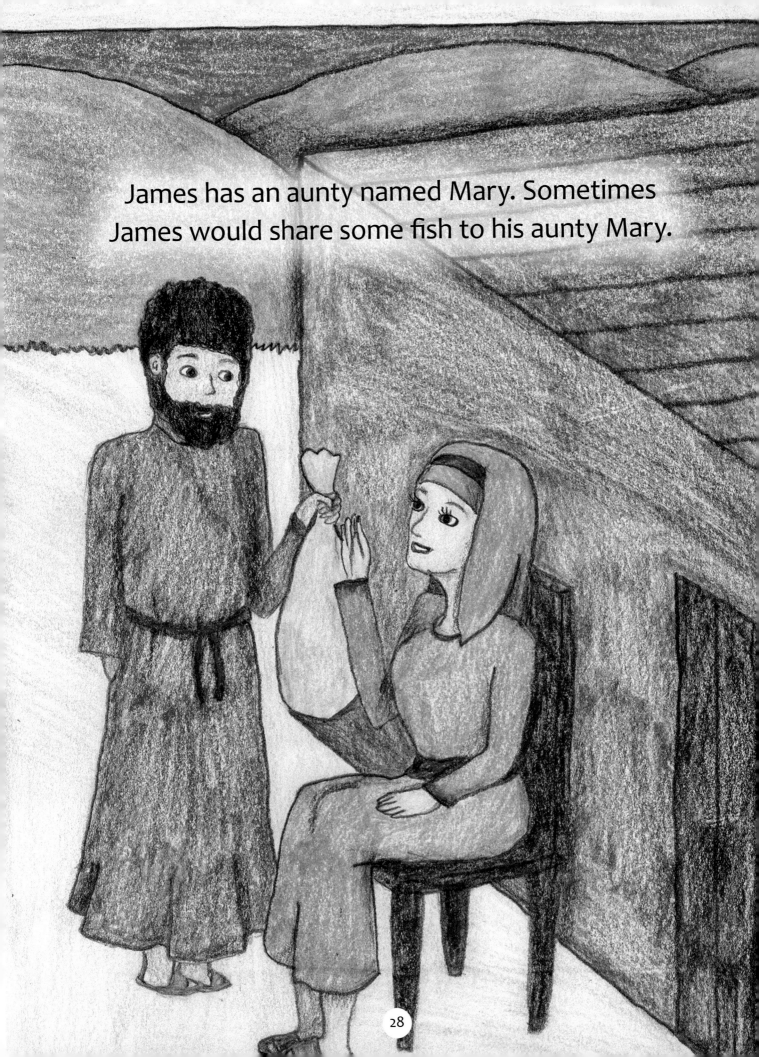

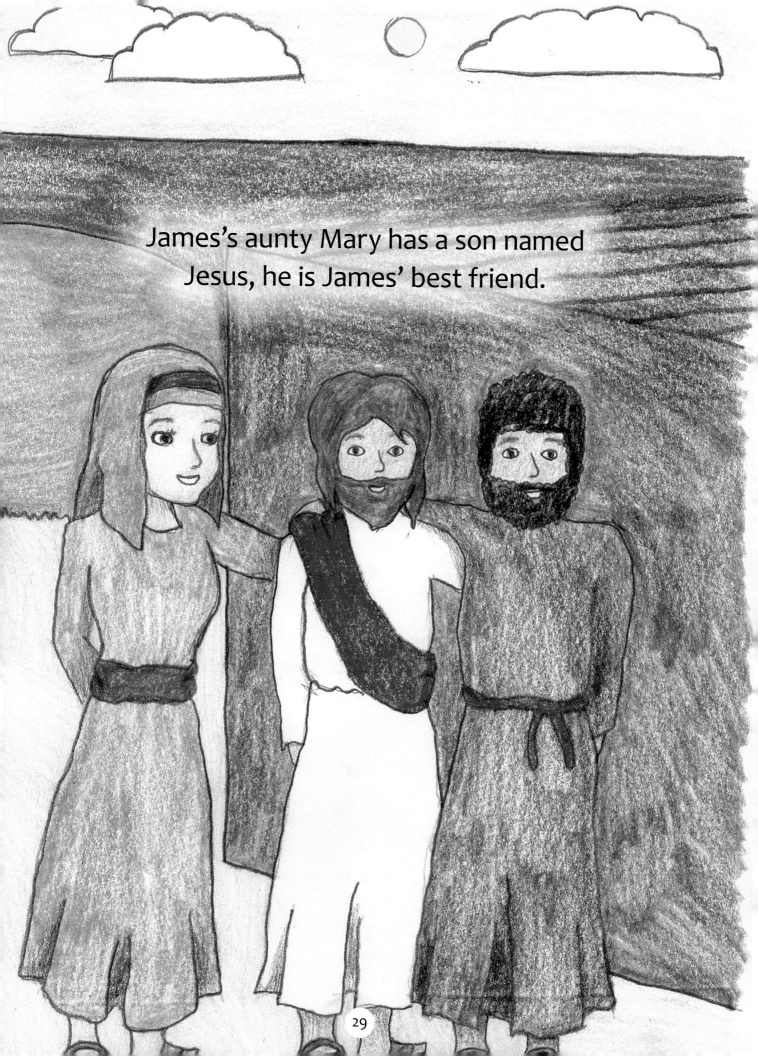

James's aunty Mary has a son named Jesus, he is James' best friend.

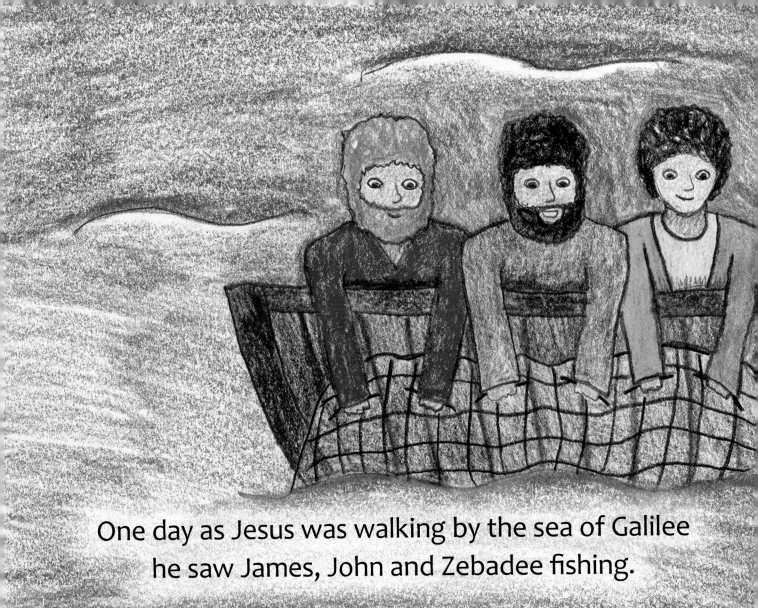

One day as Jesus was walking by the sea of Galilee he saw James, John and Zebadee fishing.

Jesus called out to James,
he immediately left the
boat, the fish and the nets
and followed Jesus.

James was the third disciples of Jesus.

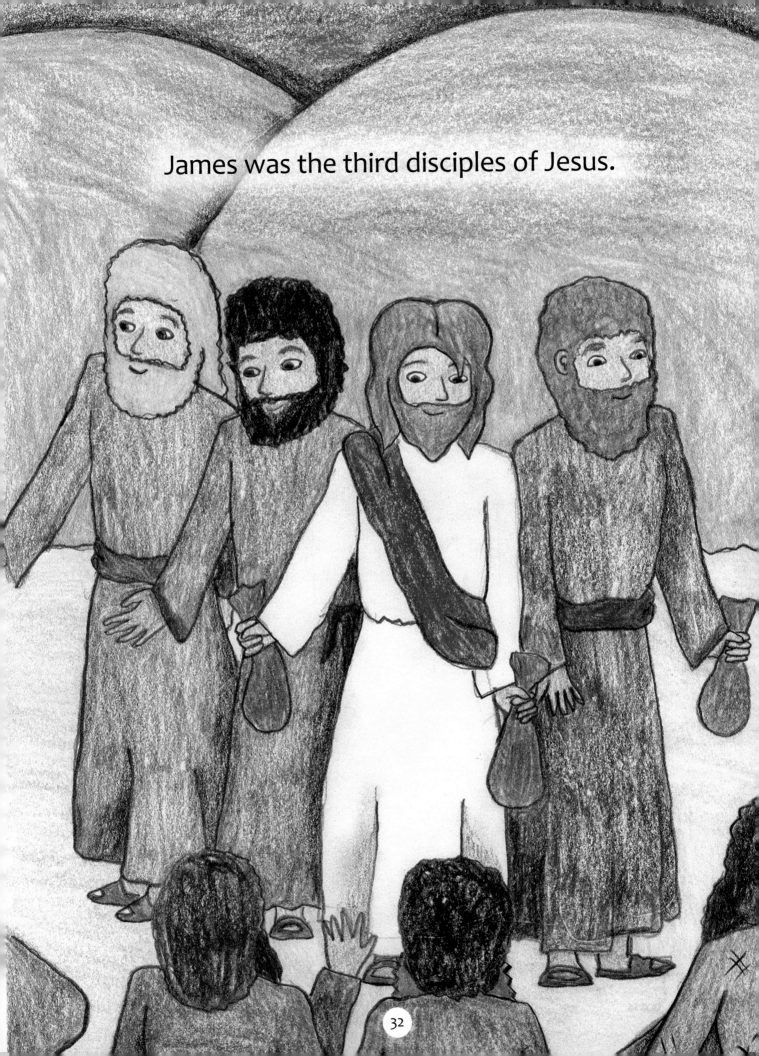

JOHN

This is John.

This is his big brother.

His name is James.

These are John's parents.

His father's name is Zebedee, and
his mother's name is Salome.

John's father is a fisherman.

He has his own fishing business.

He sells fish.

This is his father's fishing boat.

It is a big boat.

It has a lot of fishing equipment.

John always help his father and his older brother.

This is John's cousin. He is his Aunty Mary's son.

His name is Jesus.

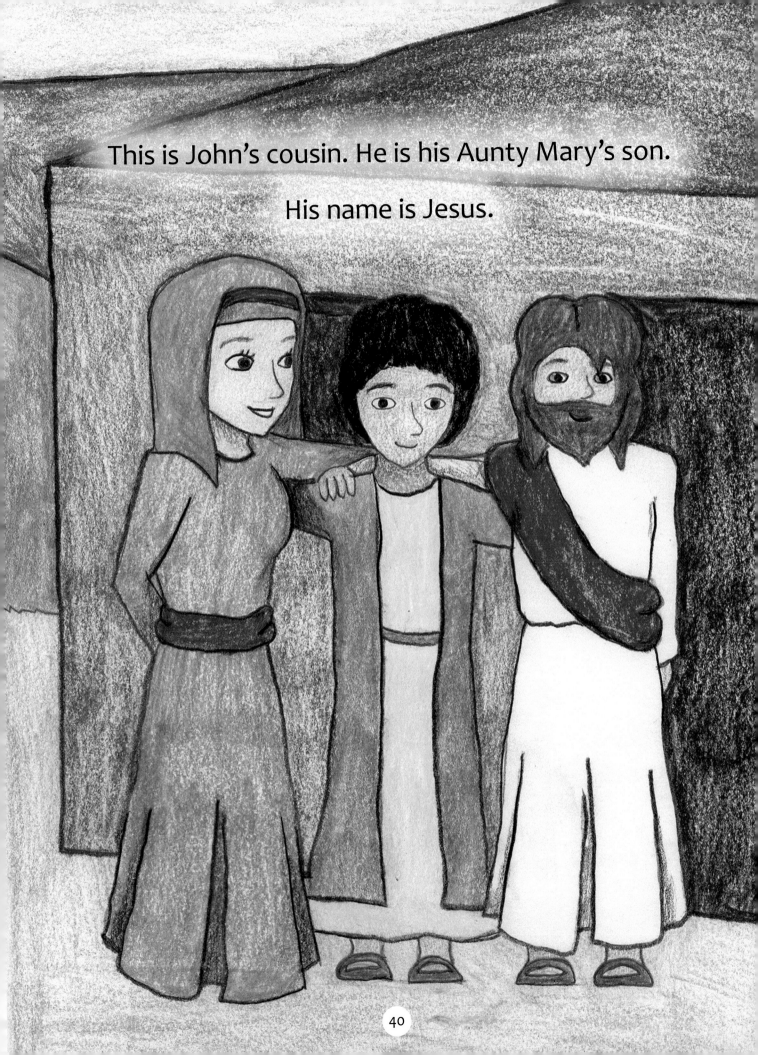

Jesus is John's best friend.

One day as Jesus was walking by the sea of Galilee, he saw John helping his father and his older brother fixing their fishing nets.

Jesus called out to John, He said, "follow me"!

Immediately John left the boat and
his father and followed Jesus.

He became one of Jesus disciples.

Now that we have known the first four disciples, we shall read the next four disciples in our next book.